Glory St. John

Weekly Reader Books presents

What
I Did
Last
Summer

ILLUSTRATED BY
EMILY ARNOLD MCCULLY

Atheneum   New York

1978

LIBRARY OF CONGRESS CATALOGING IN PUBLICATION DATA

St. John, Glory.
What I did last summer.

SUMMARY: A family disregards the use of all utilities
except water for an entire summer and lives
according to the cycle of the sun, rising at dawn and
retiring at nightfall.
[1. Family life—Fiction.   2. Camping—Fiction.
3. Energy conservation—Fiction]   I. McCully, Emily
Arnold.   II. Title.
PZ7.S1426Wh   [Fic]   78–5678
ISBN 0–689–30666–0

Book design by Mary M. Ahern

Contents

Tape 1

Off
to the
Woods!

We wanted to go camping, me and John and Elmo, but Ma couldn't take off from work and neither could Pa.

John said that we could hitchhike to the woods by ourselves, so we started packing our gear. It took us clear into the next day to get it together and tied up so that we could carry it. Then we took it all out in the backyard to figure out who'd carry what.

"It's a good thing it's Sunday," I say. "We'll get a ride quick."

"For sure," says John. "We'll be in the woods long before dark."

Elmo, he didn't say much of anything, but he sure was happy about going.

Pa came out to see how we were doing.

"Why, you boys are going to need three pack-horses to carry all that gear!" he says, slapping his leg.

Ma and Glinda and Sharon came out and stood around to see us off.

"Well, let's see," says John.

We already had on our backpacks, but there was still a heap of stuff on the ground.

"Let's see," says John again. "We *have* to take the tent and the fishin' poles."

Glinda walked over and picked up a bundle.

"You don't need a Monopoly game. Leave that at home."

"Hey, wait a minute!" I say real quick. "That's got my telescope in it, too. We'll need that, sure as shootin'!"

"What for?" asks Pa, smiling very big. "What for, Junior?"

"Why, for lookin' at the stars and the moon and the planets, of course! I can watch them all night! I *have* to take my telescope!"

Glinda laid the bundle down at the edge of the heap.

"Do you have a pan for your cooking?" asks Ma.

John and me just looked at each other. Elmo, he didn't say anything either.

"You're sure to need a frying pan to fry all those

fish you'll be catching," says Pa. We knew he was right.

"I guess we forgot about a frying pan," I say, feeling foolish, and everybody laughs.

"Here," says Ma, "I'll lend you mine." And she's off into the house to fetch it. When she's brought it out, she asks, "Which one's going to carry it? How about you, Elmo?"

Everybody laughs again, and I say, "I'll carry it for him. Here, stick it in my backpack, will you?"

Ma jammed it in, and then we all stood around, looking at that pile of stuff, just like before.

"Let's see," says John.

"Well, what do explorers do," I ask, "when they go on expeditions? They've got a lot more to carry than this."

"They've got packhorses," says Pa.

"Or extra people," says John. "Or elephants."

Pa broke up.

"That'll do it!" he says, leaning over and sort of choking. "An elephant! It'll only take one!"

I sat down and slipped off my backpack and wiped my face.

"I'm too hot to carry this thing any more," I say. "It's heavy as sin."

"But, Junior," says Pa, real serious, "you haven't even started out yet, boy! You've got to carry all this gear out to the highway to catch a ride. And then after you get to the woods, you'll have to hike till you find a campsite. You'd better get on your feet, man! You've got a good day's work ahead of you. And sure as shootin', you've got to get that tent pitched before dark!''

I looked at the sky from where I was sitting. The sun was 'way over in the afternoon.

"Oh, ghorm!" I moan and roll over on my face.

John sat down beside me. "We're not giving up," he says, firm.

"What are you going to do?" asks Sharon.

Elmo, he doesn't say anything.

"Tell you what!" says Pa, very cheerful. "Get off your face, Junior. I've got an idea."

I sat up. John slipped out of his backpack to listen better. Elmo was already listening hard.

"Well, now," says Pa. He looks around at each one of us.

Glinda and Sharon are sitting in the grass by now. Ma's got her arms folded, waiting. Her face doesn't say anything.

"Tell me what you think of this," says Pa. "These boys have got to do their camping. That's for sure."

Me and John and Elmo brightened up quick.

"We're not going to let them be disappointed, are we?" asks Pa. "Well, now. Here's my plan, and I know it'll work. We'll *all* go camping!"

John and me were up, yellin' and turnin' hand-

springs and back flips all over the place!

"Now, Pa," says Ma. "You know—"

"Just a minute, everybody!" says Pa. "Hold on! Hear me out! You'll like this, Ma. Now just listen."

We simmered down and flopped on the grass, huffin' and puffin' and punchin' each other.

"We're listening, Pa," says John. "Where are we going to camp?"

"Right here, at home!" says Pa, beaming.

"Oh, no!" we groan, me and John and Sharon and Glinda.

"I knew there was a catch," I say.

"No catch," says Pa. "You're ignorant, but you'll learn. And I'll even lay a bet with you boys. Two pairs of snowshoes says you won't be disappointed, come the end of summer!"

"Well, how in the world can that be?" I ask, thinking of the snowshoes.

"Easy," says Pa. "You boys unpack your tent and pitch it back there behind the blackberry bushes, where nobody can see it. You fellas will get to sleep out here. The rest of us will have to sleep in the house."

Ma reached for her frying pan and carried it in to the kitchen to start dinner.

Tape 2

Life in the Rough

Well, it worked. Just like Pa said it would. I wouldn't have believed it, and neither would John nor Elmo nor any of the rest. But it did. It worked.

First off, the next day a man came from the telephone company. He got out his pliers and his screwdriver that he carries in loops in his workpants. And then he does some things quick and he's got the phone loose. He winds up the cord and off he goes. Gets in his truck and drives away.

"Oh, Ma!" screams Glinda. "What'll I do? George can't call me, nor Jeannie, nor anybody! That man just pulled out our telephone!"

Ma calmed her down and explained how it was all a part of the camping. How nobody ever has a telephone at a campsite.

"But I don't give a hoot about camping!" wails Glinda. "That's for John and Junior."

"Well, Glinda," says Ma, real patient, "we aren't disappointing the boys. You yourself heard your Pa say it. Stop thinking about just yourself. Your friends aren't going to forget you. You know that."

Glinda simmered down, but she still looked like the man had pulled that telephone cord right out of her instead of the wall.

No sooner had it got quiet again than the dogs next door started in yapping at the top of their voices. John and me, we could hear Mrs. Bailey telling some man how he had the wrong house. Right off, our doorbell rang.

Sharon answered it and then she went back to the washing machine, where Ma was. Ma went to the door, drying her hands on her apron.

"Oh, yes," she says, "that's right! Go right ahead!"

Round the corner of the house came this big fella, making straight for the meter box. He wrote down something in a thick little book he had. Then he did something with a gizmo, and all the clocks on the meter stopped all at once.

"Hey!" says John.

He ran into the kitchen and pulled the light cord over the sink. The light didn't go on. He pulled it again and again. Nothing happened.

"Hey, wait a minute!" yells John, running out of the house. But the man was gone.

"He went thataway," I say.

"He turned the electricity off!" shouts John. "Now the TV won't go on!"

Ma came to the back door.

"Oh, now, you don't have TV when you're camping, you know. Your Pa promised you that you weren't going to be disappointed. Remember? Now you boys come here and help me carry this wet wash to the bathtub. We don't have any electric washing machine either when we camp."

Ma got a couple of pails, and John and me, we loaded the wash in and carried it to the bathtub.

Ma ran some water into the bathtub, enough to cover the wash, adding a little more soap too, and then she took a plumber's friend, one of those plungers, you know, out of the closet. She handed it to John.

"What's this for?" he asks.

"To agitate the wash. You plunge it up and down. Like this. Like a washing machine."

Ma showed him what she meant, and John took to it, real enthusiastic.

"Just don't splash water all over the room," says Ma. "We're washing only the clothes."

John and me, we got the dirt out of those clothes in a hurry.

Then Ma took us out to the woodshed and had me climb up and hand down the old wringer that Grandma used before she got a washer. John, he hauled out the old tub that went with it. Ma had us wash it out with the hose, and then John and me carried everything into the house for her.

We got it all set up, and it's very interesting how a wringer works. You turn a crank. Sometimes it sticks, and you have to give it a yank. We fixed that with some oil. You turn the crank, and these two rollers start rolling in *different* directions!

John and me took turns turning, and Ma pushed the wet wash through, and the sheets and towels and blue jeans and everything came out flat as pancakes, ready for the dryer.

"No dryer," says Ma. "Remember? We'll put up the old clothesline in the backyard."

Me and John found the clothesline, and it was too short. We'd been cutting pieces off for this and that whenever we needed rope. Ma rummaged around in the woodshed and came up with some more rope that me and John tied on, and it was long enough.

Ma found some clothespins and was happy as a lark that she could hang her wash out in the sunshine. The girls came out and helped, and in a minute or two everything was all hung up.

"Now that's all we have to do," says Ma. "The

sun does the rest." You could see she really liked camping!

Sharon came back from the front door and said there was another man who wanted to disconnect something.

"We've been disconnected," says John. "Twice already."

But Ma went and talked to him anyhow, and they came up with something new to disconnect.

She brought him back to the furnace room.

"Right in there," says Ma, opening the door for him.

"Let him turn it off," I say. "We don't need a furnace in the summertime. Go ahead and turn the gas off. What would we use it for anyway?"

"Hot water, stupid!" snaps Glinda, glaring in my direction. "Now we'll have to take cold showers!"

"That won't hurt you," says John. "I take cold showers all the time. Besides we're lucky to have showers at all when we're camping!"

"Oh, you and your camping! Wait till you want your dinner!" And she stamps off.

"What did she mean by that?" asks John. "What difference does dinner make?"

"The stove," says Sharon. "We can't cook without gas."

"Oh, yes, we can!" says Ma, coming out of the furnace room. "We have the Coleman!"

"What's that?"

"Why, it's a camp stove! We used to use it when the power went off. When we had that electric stove."

"I don't remember," says John.

"I do," says Sharon. "We had to pump it up to start it."

"Sounds interesting," I say. "Where do you keep it, Ma?"

"Over in the woodshed, I expect. It's been a long time since we last used it. I'm wondering if there's any fuel oil around."

Well, John and me, we started looking around the woodshed without being asked. It was getting near to dinnertime. But we didn't find any camp stove nor any fuel oil nor anything.

"Not here, Ma!" I sing out.

Ma came to the woodshed door and cast her eye about.

"I have no idea of where that stove could be," says she. "I hope your Pa didn't throw it out."

"Pa doesn't throw out anything," says Sharon. "Maybe he lent it to somebody."

"Well, it doesn't matter today," says Ma. "We have to eat what's in the refrigerator as soon as we can so that it doesn't spoil, now that the electricity is off. Tomorrow morning you boys can haul some ice from Mr. Ellis's. Tonight we'll have a cold dinner. It's hotter than usual today, so maybe your Pa won't mind." And she went in.

"I'll make a chef's salad," says Sharon.

"Whatever that is," says John.

"It's cold meat and cheese cut up in a salad with tomatoes and cucumbers and other salad things."

"We've got no cold meat," I say. "We've got no meat. I looked."

"Cheese, maybe," says Sharon, going into the kitchen.

"Baked beans'd be good," I say.

"Are you dreaming?" asks John. "How can you bake beans if you don't have a stove?"

"In the ground. Don't you know? In a hole in the ground. You line it with rocks and you build a fire there in the hole to get the rocks hot. Then you put in a pot of beans and cover it all over with dirt to hold the heat in."

"Well, I just hope you've got a lid on that pot," says John, "before you start shovelin' the dirt in on top of it!"

"Of course," I say. "Let's find some rocks. We'll fix a real camping dinner, we will!"

Well, we found some rocks, and we dug a good hole and lined it with the rocks. Everything was going along fine.

"Ma! Look!" we heard Glinda say. "Those boys have a fire out there! I see smoke!"

"John!" calls Ma. "JUNIOR!"

I went in quick.

"Look, Ma! What Mrs. Bailey handed over the fence from her garden! Fresh-pulled radishes!"

"Just what I need," says Sharon, "for the salad!"

I ran out the door.

"Just a minute here, young man!" calls Ma. "What's that smoke out there coming from?"

"Just a fire," I say

"What are you doing with a fire?"

"Well, Ma, we're cooking you some beans for dinner."

"Beans? Were'd you get beans? Mrs. Bailey?"

"No, Ma. We don't have any beans yet. But we were figuring on getting some."

"Where?"

"In the cupboard."

"Why, that's the best idea yet!" says Ma. "You'll need two big cans. Here!"

"But we were figuring on baking baked beans in the bean pot," I say.

"My land, boy," says Ma, "not for tonight! You have to start them the night before!"

"You mean cook 'em all night?"

"I mean soak them in water all night, dearie. Surely you've seen beans soaking overnight in this kitchen!"

"Oh," I say. "For baking?"

"For any kind of cooking. First off, you have to soak them. Put the water back in them, you know. They're dried, you see. You have to soften them up so that you can cook them. Come here, Junior. How did you get so dirty?"

"Diggin' the hole," I explain. "For the fire. It's a good fire, Ma. You ought to see it!"

So Ma came out. I could see that she was impressed.

"How did you find out how to do that?" she asks.

"In the camping book at the library," I say. "I was reading it all winter to get ready for our camping trip."

"Well," she says, "it's a wonder! Pop the bean pot in, why don't you?"

I'd forgotten it, so I ran back to the kitchen, opened the two big cans of beans, and dumped them into the bean pot. Then I carried it out to the bean fire.

John was prying up the top rock with a stick. Ever so careful, I set the bean pot in. John let down the hot rock on top of the beans. Then me and John made the dirt fly, piling it back on top of the smoking rocks! We made a good round pile of dirt over the beans.

"What are you boys doing there?" calls Mrs. Bailey.

Ma went over to tell her and to thank her for the

radishes, and they got to talking about gardening.

Me and John, we were watching the beans cook.

"Feel the dirt here," says John. "It's getting warm."

I felt.

"I don't feel anything warm," I say. "Maybe over here, though."

We were barefoot, so we started walking over our bean stove, trying to feel the heat with our feet.

"What in blazes are you boys doing?" we heard Pa say. "Stamping out an ant hill with your bare feet?"

"Pa! Pa!"

We started running to him. "Take off your shoes and socks and come feel it! You can feel the heat comin' right through!"

"Are you boys crazy about ant bites or just plain crazy?"

John fell over in the grass laughing, so I had to explain. Pa got very interested. He felt the dirt and said that the beans were nearly ready to eat.

I ran over to fetch Ma. Mrs. Bailey was urging her to take some tomato plants. Ma said she'd be back in the morning and then she came hurrying home.

Glinda had spread out a tablecloth on the grass and brought dishes and forks and knives out. Sharon brought out the salad and the bread and butter. We all sat in the grass and gave thanks, and me and

John, we sat nearest to the bean stove.

"Well, this is a real camping dinner!" says Ma. "And John and Junior are the cooks!"

"When are we going to get to eat this underground dinner?" asks Pa.

Me and John, we jumped up.

"Just a minute, men," says Pa. "Junior, you run in and fetch Ma's pot-lifting mitts to protect your hands. John, when you start digging out those beans, be careful! We don't care for dirt in our plates."

I got back with the mitts just in time to help John shove aside the top rock.

There sat the bean pot in the hole, black as soot and pipin' hot! Wearing the mitts, I lifted out the hot bean pot. Then I took off the lid, and we could see the beans sizzling inside.

Pa officiated with the serving spoon and filled up all our plates. Ma said they were the very best beans she's ever eaten in all her life! Me, I piled on the bread and butter and didn't have much need of salad. I filled in the cracks with milk and lay back.

"Tonight," says Ma, "I'll put some dried beans to soak, and you can bake them in your underground camp stove tomorrow."

"Let's use some soybeans too, Ma," says Sharon.

"Well, they taste different," says Ma. "Do you like them as well?"

"Oh, yes!" Sharon says. "And they're as good as meat for you. They have all the amino acids in them that you need."

"Whatever they may be," says Pa.

"They're protein, like in meat. Even if meat's too high, we can still eat lots of protein in soybeans."

"And just in case we get tired of beans," says Pa, "I have something else up my sleeve. John, come give me a hand."

Me and John, we both went to help Pa get whatever it was out of his sleeve. We went round front, and Pa hauled open the trunk of the car.

"This," he says, pointing to a green metal case. "Carry it carefully."

"What is it, Pa?"

"Something to please your Ma," he says. "Now take it easy and watch where you're going." Then he picked up a big can with a handle on it and slammed down the trunk lid.

We carried it, bein' very careful. It was heavy, like it had metal inside.

"What do you think it is?" I ask John. We're turning the corner of the house now.

"The Coleman!" cries Ma and comes running over. "Oh, Pa, we looked everywhere for it!"

"Set it down here, boys," says Pa, and he opened it up, unfolding the top and the sides. "I cleaned it up," he says, proud. "Didn't think you'd figure a way to cook dinner without it." He tousled our heads, mine and John's.

"Can I pump it up, Pa?" I ask before John gets a chance.

"Both of you come in, and I'll show you how," says Pa. "It's a very exacting process."

So he showed us how to take the tank out and fill it with oil and turn the pins right and pump the air in and all. Then he lighted it and adjusted it until it glowed all blue! Beautiful!

"She's all set to go," says Pa and turned it off.

"All ready for hot tea in the morning," says Ma. "Now aren't we lucky to have such an easy time of it when we're camping?"

"Oh, that reminds me," says Pa. "Come on out, everybody, and let's decide something."

We all went out and sat around.

"Now most people when they're camping," says Pa, "they carry their water from a pump somewhere or a spring or a clear stream. But we don't have any pump nor stream nor spring. I was just wondering," he says, looking around. "Would you mind awfully much if we just left the water connected and turned it on out of the tap?"

"Well, I think it's up to the boys to decide," says Ma. "They're the ones who are the camping experts."

Pa turned to me and John.

"How about it?" he asks.

"Sure, Pa!"

"That's all right with me!"

We answered right on top of each other. We were both thinking we could probably pull through without carrying the buckets and the pump and all.

"After all," I say, "it *is* good and cold, the water is."

"Well, that's good," says Pa. "I was a little worried. It was the only part I couldn't fix up like a campsite." He smiled as if he didn't have to worry any more. "Did they turn off the electricity today?"

"*And* the telephone," says Glinda.

"I like the quiet," says Ma. "I don't have to jump up and answer it a hundred times a day."

"It's getting dark," says Sharon. "Look how beautiful—the way the stars come out, one at a time. You can't see them when the lights are all turned on. You don't hear the dark then either. Not like now. Listen! Hear the crickets?"

"Those are tree frogs," I say. "Think I'll be gettin' back to the tent to see Elmo. He sure is enjoying the camping!"

"Good night," says Ma. "Don't let the tree frogs bite."

"Good night," say me and John.

That was the night that things began to happen.

Tape 3

Attack!

There was a full moon that night.

Funny how hard it is to sleep when the moon is bright. Especially if you're sleeping outdoors.

Lying there in the bright darkness, I got to wondering about all kinds of things and why they are and why they aren't. I could hear leaves rustling and faraway noises humming and clonking.

Then there was this little noise up close, rustling now and then.

Maybe a dog, I think.

But Mrs Bailey keeps her dogs locked in the house at night. And she's got a fence around her yard. Still that noise was sure as shootin' in Mrs. Bailey's garden.

I pushed up on one elbow to listen better.

John and Elmo were out cold. Not making a sound. Not making a breath that you could hear.

I couldn't see anything out through the tent door, so I crept outside. The rustling stopped, I waited till it began again. Sure enough, it *was* on the other side of Mrs. Bailey's fence. After a minute or two I could see some garden plants moving in the moonlight.

A coon! A coon has got under the fence somewhere, I think, and it's eating up Mrs. Bailey's choice vegetables!

I started feeling around for something to throw to scare it away. My hand lighted on a stone. I shot it into the middle of the twitching bean poles. *Wump!*

The coon stopped dead. Not a sound. Not a rustle.

Did I hit him? Maybe I killed him! Poor little fella's lying there with his feet up in the air and his little eyes closed. I didn't mean to hurt him. Just wanted to scare him.

I lobbed a pebble over lightly to see if he still had any life in him. Just to get a reaction.

Well, I'm here to say that I got my reaction! There was still plenty of life in him!

First off, this strong lemon smell. Sure was gatherin' strength! Sure was—Hey! Wait a minute! *That's* no coon!

I turned tail and ran, but it was too late. I tripped

over the tent ropes and went sprawling. The tent began to collapse. John was making some muffled sounds.

"Hey! *Hey!* We're bein' attacked by skunks! Junior! *Quick!* Come on! Let's get outta here!"

He came tumblin' out from under the tent.

"They're pullin' the tent down! Get out, Junior! Ack! The smell is awful!"

He jumped up and stumbled into me. Then he gave a tre*men*dous leap and sailed clear over me, making for the kitchen door.

I went limping after him, but as soon as I got in the kitchen door, he shoved me out and locked it.

We were trying to be quiet so as not to wake everybody up. Next thing I knew, John opened a window and handed out a bottle.

"Hurry up! Take it!" he whispers desperate-like. Then he shut the window down tight and locked it.

I knew what it was. The vinegar bottle. I began pouring it out in my hand and rubbing it all over me. I'd gone to sleep in my clothes, so they were stricken too. I took them off and rolled them up and poked them up in a tree as high as I could reach. I tried to make the vinegar last as best I could, using every drop of it. I poured the last of it into my hair, hoping that would take care of the smell.

Then I went back to the kitchen door, but it was

still locked. I tried every window that wasn't some-body's bedroom. But John had shut them all and locked them tight.

I was shivering by now and thinking about how to get warm. Finally I went back to the fallen-down tent, where it smelled worst of all. I hauled out a blanket and shook it hard to try to freshen it up. I also hauled out Elmo, and we went to the farthest corner of the backyard from the tent.

My hands smelled worst of anything. I wished I could take them off. I stretched them out as far away from me as I could get them, rolled the rest of me up in the blanket, and went to sleep.

I guess it was the morning light that woke me.

I got up and wrapped the blanket around me again and went back to survey the wreckage. The tent was loaded. We'd have to let it air out for ages. I groaned and sat down, but the smell drove me away.

The sky was only dimly light. A few stars were hanging on here and there, so I held my breath and crept into the tent and hauled out my telescope.

I'd been fixin' to get a stand for my telescope to hold it steady, but I didn't have one yet. Usually I prop it on anything handy. This time I just lay down on my back and sort of braced it on my nose.

I did this for a while until the stars were all gone

and my arms were shaking and my nose was all worn out. Then just as I was thinking about unlocking my muscles and lowering the telescope, something bright shot right across my line of vision!

I lowered the telescope and looked quick with my bare eyes, but it was gone.

Well, what could it have been?

I've always hoped that I could discover a comet or something like that. Maybe it's a meteor, I think.

Just then something grabbed me around the ankles. It was a second or two before I knew it was John. He'd snuk up on me.

"Hey, watch out for the telescope!" I say.

"No danger," says he, withdrawing. "The wind just changed."

I'd forgotten all about the skunk attack.

"Gettin' better, though, don't you think?"

"Not for me," he says.

"I'll bet you don't smell so good yourself."

"Listen, why don't you go take a shower before the rest of 'em get up?" suggests John.

So I stowed my telescope and hung up my blanket on the clothesline and went in. The sky was just turning bright pink.

Retreat

to

a Nearby

Galaxy

"But, John," I say, "what in thunder do you think it could have been?"

We were lying in the warm grass. The sun was just right, not too hot. We were resting from all the work of cleaning up. Our clothes and bedding were hanging on the line, all washed and wrung out. Everything from inside the tent was spread out on the grass in the sun, airing. We'd scrubbed the tent with vinegar, moved it to a new place, and hauled it up tight again. Pa said we were quarantined to the backyard till we were completely aired out.

By now it wasn't all that bad, lying in the sun, like I said.

"So what do you think it was?" I ask again, giving John a punch.

"I've got a good idea of what it was," he says mysterious-like. He rolled over and punched me back. "Funny you didn't think of it first off."

"Well, what?" I say, punching him back.

"A flying saucer, of course."

I sat up.

"Of *course!* That's why it shot off so fast! They always disappear like that! And silent!"

We both stared up into the sky.

"How do you suppose they move like that?" I ask.

"Solar energy," says John. "They've got some way of catching energy from the sun and storing it. They store it up so's they can fly down at night and investigate the Earth. If the energy supply runs low, they just fly up out of the shadow of the Earth and catch some more. It's very simple."

"But *how* do they catch it?"

"Well, that's a good question," says John. "We're catching some right now, lyin' here in the sun."

"You're going to catch it from Pa if you don't get up and mow this lawn," says Sharon, coming up with a plate of sandwiches.

"Good grief, Sharon! We just finished a week of work! I guess we can rest a little. Besides we're figurin' out something important," I say, helping myself to a sandwich.

"What?"

"How to catch solar energy."

"The ultraviolet rays from the sun are making Vitamin D in your skin, for one thing," says Sharon.

"That's very interesting," I say. "I wonder how."

"Plants can do it," says John. "Plants can do it fine. Take up the sunlight and store the energy."

"They have chlorophyll," says Sharon.

"Whatever that may be."

"That's the green stuff in the plants that makes 'em green."

"But *how* do they do it?"

"I don't know," says Sharon. "Ask them." And she goes off, leaving the sandwiches.

"That must be why the little green people from outer space are green," says John.

"Suppose we paint ourselves green," I say. "Do you think we could catch energy from the sun?"

"Good idea," says John. "Let's try it!"

We worked on the sandwiches awhile, thinking about where we could get some green coloring.

"I know!" I say. "Ma's got some green food coloring in the kitchen cabinet!"

I took the empty sandwich plate back to the kitchen and snitched the green food coloring.

We stripped to our cutoffs and smeared it all over

us. I did John's back, and he did mine. By the time we got to our feet, it was almost gone. We finished it up, rinsing out the bottle to get the very last drops. My left foot was fairly pale.

John hauled out the lawnmower, while I moved our stuff that was spread out in the sun. Then we made the grass fly!

"There's one good thing about being quarantined to the backyard," I say. "We don't have to mow the front yard!"

We raked up the grass cuttings. Then we rolled in them to add to our green color.

"Listen!" I say. "I've got a great idea! Let's outfit the tent like a flying saucer. We can take off in it, spend a few days in outer space, and when we come back, the smell will all be gone!"

"Hey, let's do it!" yells John. He looked pretty funny—all green and jumping around like a grasshopper.

So we started thinking about what we'd need in outer space.

"My telescope," I say right off. "Like Skylab."

"And the Monopoly game and the checkerboard and a deck of cards and our space guns and a new flashlight battery," says John.

"And all the cookies and crackers Ma will let us have."

34

"Peanut butter."

"For sure, and pickles."

"Outer space?" says Ma when we told her. "Why that's a dandy idea! What sort of provisions do you plan on taking?"

We told her, and she let us have everything we wanted plus a box of raisins and some oranges and apples too. It was lucky that we talked to Ma when we did, because five minutes later she was gone. Mrs. Ralston was giving a dinner party, and Ma always helps her. Ma's been Mrs. Ralston's cook ever since I can remember.

"When are you planning on lifting off?" asks Sharon.

"After dinner," says John.

"Dinner," says Sharon. "That reminds me. We'll have to get the beans baking. You boys had better start your fire in the bean hole."

"But we just finished lunch."

"I know, but these beans have to bake three or four hours. They aren't precooked like the ones last night."

So John and me, we built a good fire in the bean hole and put the bean pot in. This time we had wrapped the pot in aluminum foil. That's so when it turned black with soot from the fire, we could peel off the foil and wouldn't have to scrub off the black, like we did the night before. We covered it over with dirt, and then we retired to our Flying Saucer to plan our trip.

"First," says John, "we've got to decide where we're going."

"No place close," I say. "I'm for going to another galaxy."

"Which one?" asks John, willing.

"Well, why don't we discover one?" I say. "We can give it a name after we find it."

"Why *not!*" says John. "Our very own galaxy!"

"Green yet," says Pa when he laid eyes on us. "Is it mold, or is it jealousy?"

"Neither, Pa! It's to catch energy from the sun, like space people do," I tell him.

"And like plants do," put in John, "with chlorophyll."

"Chlorophyll?" says Pa, showing interest. "You boys may just have backed into something fairly intelligent. Chlorophyll is one very good way of getting rid of bad odors." And he went in.

Sharon came out and filled a bowl from the bean pot.

"Pa says he'd prefer to eat in the house tonight," she says. "He's not as used to the smell as the rest of us. You boys can have what's left of the beans. I'll bring you out tomatoes and dessert and milk."

Sharon had cut up some sausage into the beans, and they were mighty tasty. Me and John filled up ourselves twice, and there were still more beans left over.

"We'd better take them with us on the Flying Saucer," says John. "The more provisions, the better."

So we loaded them in. The Saucer was looking real shipshape by now.

"Have we got everything?" asks John. "Anything else we need before we lift off?"

It was getting dark. We were fastening on our space helmets.

"Hey, where's Elmo?" I say all of a sudden. I ran to the part of the backyard where I'd taken him after the skunk attack, but he wasn't there. We got out the flashlight and looked everywhere.

"It was the smell drove him away," says John. "He couldn't hack it."

"But we've *got* to find him before lift-off!" I say. "He'll miss discoverin' our new galaxy!"

Sharon came out of the darkness.

"I've come to see you lift off," she says. "Pa and Glinda say to give you their congratulations, but they can't make it. And Ma isn't home yet."

"We've lost Elmo!" I say. "We can't go without him!"

"Maybe he doesn't like space travel," says Sharon.

"Maybe he's too polite to come right out and say it."

"She's right," says John. "It would be too hard on him, the pressure and all." I knew they were both right.

I hated to leave Elmo behind, but there was nothing else to do.

We climbed into the Saucer, zipped the door tight, and got ready to lift off.

"All systems AOK!" shouts John. He was manning the flight controls. I was manning the generator.

I counted down, and Sharon stood outside, calling good-bye.

"Ten! Nine! Eight!"

"Good-bye, John! Good-bye, Junior!"

Sssssssssssssssss!

"Seven! Six!"

"Good luck!"

"Four! Three! Two!"

Mmmmmmmm—

"Good-bye!"

"One!"

"Lift off!"

With a tremendous bunch of light and in utter silence, the Saucer lifted away from little Earth into the black of awful Space!

Far below us, Sharon was still wavin'.

Tape 5

The
Space
Snake
Strikes!

Well, we finally left the solar system that Earth belongs to. We had to pass Mars and Jupiter and all the rest. Jupiter was really big, and so was Saturn. But we finally got free of our Sun and its planets. Then we set our course straight out of our galaxy to get free of *it*.

"Think I'll take a space walk and get our bearings," I say after a while.

"Don't forget your tether," says John.

I tied a rope around my waist and secured the other end of it to the Saucer. Then I stepped outside.

I wasn't prepared for the amazing and really beautiful sight that met my eyes!

There, strung out across space was our old galaxy, like a giant wheel! Millions and billions of suns shone out of it like little dots of pepper. I was looking at the wheel on edge, and it stretched across Space as far as I could see.

"Hey, John!" I call. "Set the controls on automatic and come take a look at this!"

So John tethered himself and came on out.

"Look at that!" I say, pointing.

He looks.

"What is it?" he asks after a while. "Some kind of star somewhere? What am I supposed to be lookin' at?"

"The galaxy, you turkey! See right across the sky —that big arch of stars?"

"Oh, you mean the Milky Way?"

"Yes, but we're looking at it from the outside! That's our galaxy, all right, but we're outside it, lookin' back! We made it out!"

"We did?" asks John in amazement.

"Absolutely," I say. "We're on the outside, lookin' back at it! Isn't that the most amazing and terrific sight you've ever seen?"

Then John began to grasp what it was that we had done. He clapped me on the back.

"You're a great navigator!" he says to me.

"And you're a great pilot!" I say to him, clapping him on the back. "We did it!"

Then we started in punchin' each other, and our tethers got tangled, and we had to recall that we were out in space treading on less than air.

"Good grief!" says John, sitting down on some space. "I'm about worn out from piloting this Flying Saucer out of the galaxy! Think I'll leave her on automatic and sack out."

"Me too," I say.

So we made it back into the Saucer and passed out, too dead tired even to talk. It's very exhausting, finding your way out of the galaxy.

When we woke up, we had entered the atmosphere of a planet that seemed to be all water. We set the Saucer down, silent-like, and held a conference.

"I vote for Monopoly," says John.

"I vote for chow," I say.

So we broke out some rations. By the time we were through, we had eaten all the cookies and half the oranges and some pickles. But we couldn't find the Monopoly game.

"Must have left it back on Earth," I say. "Never mind. I've got something better."

"I hope it's cheese crackers," says John. He's real fond of cheese crackers. Pa says he has a mad passion for them.

"No," I say, "but it's close to *cheese*."

"Milk? *Ice* cream?"

"Nothing to eat," I say. "The name of it is close to *cheese*. That's what I meant. It's a game."

"I give up," says John.

"Chess!" I say and break out the checkerboard.

"But I don't know how to play chess," says John.

"Don't worry," I say. "I'll teach you. Bill Dwyer left his chessmen with me while he went to California. Me and Bill, we played all last winter, whenever I went to his house. It's very interesting. Better than checkers."

"It'd better be," says John, grumpy.

While I was rummaging around, I found some cheese crackers. That cheered John up. Then I found the chessmen. That cheered me up.

"Chess is a battle game," I say. "Considering our position just now, shouldn't we make it a Space Battle? All the chessmen could be spacemen."

We set up the board, and I showed John where the spacemen went and how they moved.

"Let's have a Space War between two galaxies," says John. "Mine's going to be the Pole Star Galaxy."

"That's got to be our old galaxy, back where Earth is. That's where the Pole Star is."

"OK by me," says John. "What's your galaxy?"

I thought for a minute. "Well, in that case, I guess mine'll have to be the Pole *Cat* Galaxy!"

So we fought all morning.

"The Skunks are marching, one by one," I chant. "The Skunks are coming to make you run!" I zoomed a Space Knight through John's front line. "Check!"

John's Space King retreated.

"The Skunks are coming, two by two. The Skunks are coming to skunk on *you!*" And I pulled up my Space Queen.

"Pole Stars are shining, three by three. Pole Stars are shining to *de*fend *me!*" sings out John, capturing my Space Knight with a Space Pawn.

"Ow!" I squawk. "I didn't see that." My Space Queen withdraws in a hurry behind a Space Castle.

"Pole Stars are comin', four by four! They're comin' to give you some more war!" And John advances his Space Bishop.

"The Skunks are coming, five by five, to see if you are still alive!" I shot my Space Queen in behind his Space Bishop. "Check!" I had him. His Space Bishop was dead.

He moved his Space King to safety, and I captured his Space Bishop. I also pinned his Space Queen.

"The Skunks are coming, six feet tall! There'll be nothing left of you at all!"

Well, it was fun. The Pole Cat Galaxy and the Pole Star Galaxy crashed and collided over and over again, slashing and smashing and passing each other. When the smoke cleared away, I had won three games, and John had won two. He was catching on fast.

"I'm thirsty," I say.

John gives me a funny, blank look.

"We didn't bring a drop to drink," he says, as if he can't believe what he's saying.

I looked at John. I couldn't believe it either.

"Well," I say, "there's nothing to do but set out a pan to catch some of the watery atmosphere that this Water Planet is dropping all around us."

But we didn't have a pan.

"Nothing but the bean pot," says John.

So we ate the rest of the beans, and luckily they were nice and juicy. Then we set the empty bean pot outside the Saucer in the watery atmosphere that was coming down all around us.

"Hope it fills up fast," I say, "before we die of thirst."

It didn't fill up fast. We took turns drinking the drops as they collected. They tasted like beans. Then we lay on our backs with our heads sticking out the door of the Saucer and our mouths open as wide as we could get them.

"Two drops," says John.

"Three," I say.

"Four, five, six," he says.

We went on like this for a while, and then I noticed something.

"Hey, your face isn't so green any more!"

John wiped his face and looked at his hand.

"Maybe this Water Planet isn't so good for us. I sure don't want to lose my green color!" he says. "I won't be able to make energy from the sunlight."

"Well, we can't leave now," I say, looking at the generator gauges. "We're out of fuel till the sun comes out."

"Maybe it'll never come out. Maybe this is a planet with a tremendous thick cloud of water vapor around it, and the sunlight never gets through."

"In that case," I say, "we'll have to split the water into hydrogen and oxygen and use the hydrogen for fuel. I'd better get the equipment ready."

We decided not to leave just yet because it was sort of homey and nice inside the Saucer. We played Black Jack and ate all the apples and some of the raisins and the rest of the crackers.

"We haven't named this planet that we've discovered," I remind John.

"Oh, I think Water Planet is a good name. How could we forget it?"

"Hey, and that's not all," I say, just beginning to realize where we are. "This Water Planet is in a

new galaxy! *We've discovered our galaxy!* We made
it!"

We began to yip and yell and roll around the
Saucer till it shook like four sails in a gale. After a
while we settled down and began throwing out
names for our new galaxy.

"*Intrepid,*" says John. "I like that."

"How about *Ultimate?*"

"Negative," says John. "What does it mean?"

"Something like *the best.*"

"What about the Last Galaxy?"

"Last Gasp Galaxy!" I gasp.

"That's real good," says John, "but you know
what I like best of all? Pole Cat Galaxy. It sounds
so homey. Let's name it Pole Cat Galaxy!"

So we did.

"Probably when we grow up, we'll be finding
galaxies all the time," I say, stretching back and
reaching for an orange. "We'll each have our own
little Saucer and go zooming around the Universe,
explorin' and adventurin'."

John checked our running lights. We had little
red lights that went on and off around the edge of
the Saucer. They went in one direction. Then we
had green lights that went in the other direction.
Real pretty.

I opened the door.

"Hey, the sun is out!" I shout. "Let's explore our planet!"

We put on our space helmets and took our space guns and crept out.

"Don't forget we're alien beings," whispered John. "Don't let anybody see you."

We kept behind the Water Planet bushes. They were dripping wet. Out in a clearing there was a big rock that was dry. I was all for going to the rock to sit in the sun, but John, he says that's too dangerous.

Something made me go anyway, and it was then that I saw him—stretched out on the rock in the sun! I grabbed him quick before he could get away!

"Look here! I found Elmo!"

"That can't be Elmo," says John. "He's on another planet. What you've got there is a Space Snake! Be careful!"

I looked at the Space Snake carefully.

"Funny how snakes always like me," I say. "Anywhere in Space."

I put him in a basket with a lid and left him in the sun on the rock.

"He's *got* to be a rare specimen. Nobody's ever taken a Space Snake back to Earth before."

"What makes you think we'll get back to Earth?" asks John.

"Well, why not?" I ask.

"Why, anything could happen. The Saucer might not start, or the engines might malfunction somewhere out in Space. Or we might be attacked by a whole flock of Space Snakes before we can leave this planet. Or we might catch a noxious disease never before suffered by man."

"I'm feeling kind of sick right now," I say, my knees buckling under me.

John helped me into the Saucer and laid me down, careful. I'm gaspin' and chokin' by now.

"It was the Space Snake," I gasp. "He gave me a deadly disease. Go try to find some Water Planet herbs to cure me." I fell back unconscious.

John went.

Soon as he was gone, I grabbed a red felt pen and began making red dots all over me. I fell back just in time as John came in again.

"Here's something will cure you," he says, bringing in some wet leaves.

I looked up weakly.

"Hey!" he says. "You're breaking out with something! You really are! Maybe poison ivy." He looked at his own hands and arms. Then he looked at me again. "What's the matter with you?"

"It's the Spotted Fever," I gasp. "It's deadly. You were right. We probably won't get back to Earth."

"I'd better lift off fast!" says John. "But how can we make it without a navigator?"

"Food!" I whisper. "Quick!"

John made a clean sweep of the rations. Half a box of raisins and one orange.

"Peanut butter!" I gasp.

"That's right," he says. "But where is it?"

While he was looking, I slipped outside and smuggled in the Space Snake. Then I plastered the wet leaves all over me.

John found the jar of peanut butter, and we attacked it with two spoons. After we'd polished it off, I felt greatly revived.

"I think I'll live," I say. "Any crackers left?"

"Not a one," says John. "Have some raisins."

We finished the raisins and split the orange and drank the rest of the bean water. By now the sun had set on the Water Planet, and it was nearly dark. John began checking out the Saucer system. The red and green lights were going fine.

"All systems AOK!" sings out John.

Lift-off was perfect. We left the Water Planet. We left Pole Cat Galaxy. We headed for home.

"Think I'll take a space walk," I say, tethering up.

I stepped outside, and there it was! Our own Pole Star Galaxy coming in! It stretched right across space, from one side to the other. We were coming at it from the edge, just like we'd left it.

"We're right on course," I say, entering the Saucer.

"Know what I'm going to do as soon as we get back to Earth?" asks John.

"What?"

"Drink a gallon of water."

"Know what I'm going to do?" I ask.

"No, what?"

"Build me a stand for my telescope."

"What for?"

"So I can find our Pole Cat Galaxy and look at it whenever I want. From a safe distance, that is."

The Hideout

Along about that time we had an awful heat wave. Me and John, we spent most of our time swimming, after we'd finished our camping chores. All anybody could think about was keepin' cool. One trouble was keeping cool enough to sleep. Even the tent was too hot.

"Where's John and Junior?" we heard Glinda say early one morning when she and Ma were hanging out the wash.

"Probably swimming," says Ma, "don't you suppose?"

"No," says Glinda, "because their swimming trunks are still here."

"Then I've no idea," says Ma. "Sure they aren't somewhere around?"

"Nope," says Glinda. "I've looked everywhere."

But we were. We were in the backyard. In our hideout.

"How long before they find us, do you bet?" asks John.

"Never," I say, "unless you give it away. I'm sure not going to. I like being incognito."

"Whatever that may be."

"It means nobody knows where you are."

"No, it doesn't. It means they don't know *who* you are."

"Well, if you know so much, why did you ask?" I say with a punch.

"Take it easy," he warns, "or they'll all know where we are."

Anyhow our hideout was cool. If there was a breeze goin', we had it. It was nice and shady. Besides there was a certain amount of danger. John says you always have to have some danger to really enjoy anything.

"The next step," says John, "is to make the hideout permanent."

"That'll take boards and nails."

"Let's look in the woodshed."

So we slipped down the trapeze and snuck into the woodshed when nobody was looking. We found some boards, but they were too long. We knew that if we did any sawing, then everybody would hear us.

"Well, they'll just have to hear us," says John.

"Anyway they'd hear us hammering."

"Maybe we can wait till everybody's gone somewhere."

"Fat chance."

We left the lumber for the time being and slipped outside.

The first thing that met our eyes was a big pitcher of lemonade and a plate of cookies sitting on the picnic table. Well, we couldn't let that go uninvestigated!

As soon as we began our investigation, who should pop out of the bushes but Sharon.

"Gotcha!" she says, smilin' real big. "I know how to trap you two."

"We aren't trapped," says John. "What are you talking about?"

"Yes, you are," says Sharon. "You two have been hiding out somewhere, but I trapped you. Now I know where you are."

"But you don't know where we've been hiding out."

"Of course, I do! In the woodshed. I saw you come out."

Me and John hooted and hollered and rolled in the grass. But we didn't let out a single clue. Right then and there, without saying a word, we both decided not to give away our hideout with any hammering until they found out by themselves where it was. We didn't count on Pa though.

"Where are John and Junior?" asks Pa, soon as he gets home.

"They're hiding out," says Glinda. "They've been hiding out all day. We don't know where."

"Oh?" says Pa innocent-like.

We saw him mosey out to the backyard like he was interested in the vegetable garden. Then he went back to where Sharon was setting the picnic table for dinner.

"I expect we'll see the boys," he says, "when dinner's on the table." And he went into the house.

Me and John scooted down the trapeze and ran down the alley and around the corner and came in the front door.

"Dinner ready, Ma?"

"Oh, there you are!" says Ma. "Just in time. Wash your hands."

So we did and sat down at the table with every-body else.

"I guess you boys had no trouble keeping cool today, did you?" asks Pa, lifting his eyebrows in our direction.

"No, Pa, we didn't," says John, looking sideways at me.

"How do you know, Pa?" asks Sharon.

"Cause I'm your Pa. I know everything."

"Come on, Pa. You don't. Not everything," I say.

"Name one thing," says Pa, passing me the fried potatoes.

"Where our hideout is," I say, taking up the challenge.

"You mean you want me to say right out?"

"Sure, Pa," John says. "We know you're just bluffing."

"Well, then I'm bluffing about the oak tree. You two monkeys have a hideout up in the oak leaves, where it's shady and breezy and the coolest place around."

"How'd you know?" we both say together.

"Because there was no trapeze hanging down when I went out to look at the garden. And now that you've come down, the trapeze is down. In fact, it looks to me as if you've made a sort of ladder out of it."

Me and John, we just looked at each other.

"Leave it to Pa," says John.

"I want to congratulate you," says Pa, "on using your heads. Are you going to sleep up there?"

"That's right, Pa!" I say. "As soon as we can build a tree house! We were figuring on using some of the old boards in the woodshed."

"After dinner," says Pa, "let's take a look. I think we can come up with something."

John kicked me under the table, and I almost yelped with joy!

So that's how it began—our permanent hideout.

Right after dinner Pa picked out the boards that we could use and the nails. First off, John climbed up the trapeze-ladder carrying a length of rope. Soon as he reached the first branch, he tied one end of the rope around it. Then he dropped the other end down to me. I tied it around one of the boards, and he began hauling it up.

The first time he hauled it up, the board slipped out of the rope, and I had to dodge out of the way to keep from being clobbered. But I tried again and again, and got the hang of how to tie it so that it wouldn't slip out, and up went the first board to the first branch!

We wanted to get it to the next branch up, because we would be all hidden by leaves there. But the more we tried, the more we agreed that maybe we'd better settle for the first branch. Where it divided into two branches was good and strong. It just wasn't as hidden by leaves.

"Oh, what does it matter?" John says finally. "What does it matter if people can see it? They all know we're up here anyway."

So we decided to build our hideout on the lowest branch, which really isn't low at all. Our oak tree is plenty big. The trunk is too big around to climb. That's why we have to use a rope ladder to get up. Anyway we laid the board across the two dividing

branches of the lowest branch. The board was too long.

"Let's move it a little farther out," I say.

We did, and it fit. Perfect.

"I've got the nails in my pocket," I say. "Why don't you go down and get the hammer?"

Down John went and up he came with the hammer stuck in his belt.

We nailed down both ends of the first board. Then we swung from it by our hands to see if it would hold, and it did. It was as solid as the tree.

"Let's get the other floor boards nailed down before dark," says John.

Well, we did the same over again with a second board the same length. Only this board we nailed

closer to where the branches divided, and the ends stuck out beyond the branches a little way. This second board was parallel to the first one to make the second side of a square, see? When we got the other two sides of the square up, then we'd have the outline of the floor.

But we didn't get those other boards up till the next day. The third board we nailed on first off the next morning, but the board that was the last side of the square—we didn't get it nailed down till the last thing before dinner. Because in between, we nailed down all the floorboards! Sawed them the right length and nailed 'em down!

Ma and Sharon and Glinda came out to inspect our work. Ma had baked us a cake special at Mrs. Ralston's in celebration.

We heard Pa drive up out front, and me and John, we scooted down the trapeze like real monkeys.

"Pa! Pa!" we yell, running around the house. "Come and see the floor! It's all finished!"

Pa was taking a brown paper bag out of the car. He handed it to me. It was heavy. I looked inside.

"Corner braces," says Pa, "and the screws to hold them. I figured you'd be ready to put up the walls."

"Good idea," says John. "I was wondering about the walls."

After dinner, me and John and Pa, we had a conference on how to build the rest of our tree hideout.

"We'll have to make the roof slanted, so's the rain will run off," says John.

"Roof?" says Pa. "What for? What do you need a roof for?"

"Why, to keep the rain off!"

"You'll also keep the breeze off."

"But what will we do when it rains?"

"Come down," says Pa. "Don't you have enough sense to come in out of the rain?"

"But I want to stay up in our hideout when it rains."

"Fine," says Pa. "In a gentle rain the leaves will keep you dry. In a heavy rain, you'd be much happier on the ground."

"OK," says John at last. "We won't have a roof. That will save us a lot of work."

"But we have to have walls to keep us from rolling off in our sleep," I say.

"Right," agrees Pa. "How high do you want your walls?"

John and I, we looked at each other.

"If you don't have a roof, how high are your walls?" John says.

"Maybe they should be kind of low," I say, "so as not to keep the breeze out."

"Now you're thinking," says Pa. "Why don't you get out the corner braces and take a look at them?"

So John took out the little sack with the screws

in it and handed it to Pa. Then he dumped the braces on the ground. There were sixteen of them.

"You figure out the best way to use them," says Pa, getting up. "When you're agreed, let's continue our conference."

Me and John, we worked on this till almost dark, and this is what we agreed on. A square of four boards around the bottom of the wall. A square of four boards around the top of the wall. A brace for each corner. That makes eight. Then we'd connect the bottom square and the top square with up-and-down boards, about eighteen inches high, and that would be the walls. We'd use two braces for each side and screw them to the floor. That's eight more braces, and that makes sixteen all together.

Pa thought this was a mighty good plan.

"One thing more," he says. "Why don't you run a long support to the next branch above and nail it on solid? Nail the bottom end to the branch you're building on, right at the point where you climb into your crow's nest. Then you'll have something to hang onto when you climb in and out. If you locate it so that you can bolt your wall to it too, then that will secure your wall to one strong upright, see?"

The last thing before dark, Pa showed us how to use the drill. I figured that we'd be drilling sixty-four holes!

We did it, too. The next day we built each wall separate. Then we drilled the holes where the corner braces would go. We'd already hoisted up one of the walls when Pa came home.

First thing he did was to come to the backyard to check on the Crow's Nest. We'd figured on having it finished when he got home, but he thought we'd done fine.

"Good job, men!" he says. "I couldn't have done better myself. You'll finish it before dark, I expect."

"Then we can sleep in it tonight!" I shout.

"Yippee!" yells John and does a back flip off the trapeze.

Pa was right. We did finish it before dark. Pa used the big house ladder that he gets on the roof with and he nailed the long support board onto our branch and onto the one above. Then he gave us a couple of big bolts, and we drilled the holes and bolted one side of the wall to it.

One by one, we hauled up the other three walls. We fastened them to each other and to the floorboards with the corner braces.

We were finished!

We hauled up our blankets. John ran into the house to get a skull-and-crossbones flag that he keeps on the wall of our room. We lashed it to the long support in the last of the daylight.

Then we were alone in the rustling leaves and the rippling air. When we lay down, we couldn't see the stars. We didn't stay awake to see what else we couldn't see. It seemed to me that I was in a boat, floating in the ocean, drifting through quiet waters farther and farther from shore . . .

Tape 7

The Great Fish Fry

What is it like to live up in a tree?

Well, it's quiet and rustly and green. And it's a little shaky underfoot. That's at first. After a while you don't notice those things. You notice all sorts of other things. It comes to you that you're not alone. There are a lot of others living in that tree besides you. Insects, birds, squirrels. If we didn't live in town, we might have a possum. Or even a cougar or a bear! Under the roots of the tree, we might have mice or rabbits.

John and I, we took to leaving peanuts on the railing of our Crow's Nest. In the morning the peanuts would be gone, and so would be whoever took them. Then one morning I woke up and found myself staring at a little squirrel. It wasn't full-grown. Its fur was ever so perfect, every hair in place. What had wakened me was the racket it made chewing the shell off the peanut. Always before, I guess, it had grabbed the peanuts and run. But here it was, brave as a lion, sitting up there, munching right in my face.

I didn't move till it finished eating and left. Then I put out some more peanuts. It wasn't long till the little rascal was back again. I didn't wiggle so much as a freckle, but it knew I was watching. Even so, it dared to come and grab the peanuts, one at a time. It carried them out toward the end of the branch to eat them.

Day by day, we got better acquainted, and that's how me and John made a pet of Squiffels.

Pa said it looked as if we were going to live in the oak tree the rest of our lives. He said we were going to wind up *looking* like Squiffels. When Squiff got through training us to provide his food for him, why then he'd train us to be squirrels, and we'd never come down. It's true we were having such a good time that we didn't plan on coming down till snow fell.

Then something made us change our minds in a hurry.

Pa came home one night waving a fishing pole. "Anybody around here interested in going fishing?" he asks.

Me and John, we were down the rope ladder like greased lightning.

"How soon, Pa?"

"How long can we go for?"

"How about tomorrow morning?" says Pa. "I've got Monday off. We can make it a long weekend."

Me and John started in whoopin' and hollerin'. We'd given up any hope of ever going fishing the whole summer long.

Ma and Glinda and Sharon came out to see what the fuss was about. We told them. Then Glinda and Sharon, *they* started in whoopin' and hollerin'.

"Look how glad these girls are to see us go!" says Pa. "Why do you suppose they want us out of the way?"

"So we can have our pajama party!" says Glinda. "All the girls can come over, and we can sleep in the backyard. They've been wanting to come because we can have candles instead of electric lights."

"Then we'll have a big breakfast in the morning," puts in Sharon. "We couldn't possibly do it with you here."

"What's your ma going to be doing?" asks Pa.

"Frying bacon, I expect," says Ma.

"No, you won't, Ma. You're going to take it

easy. Glinda and I are going to buy the breakfast and cook it. We've been saving our money from helping at Mrs. Ralston's parties. We've been planning this for ages and ages. Oh, I'm so glad you're going!" Sharon threw her arms around Pa and hugged him.

"Well, this has got to be the most heartfelt send-off I've ever had," says Pa. "Nobody ever came right out like this and said how happy they were that I was leaving!"

"It appears your Pa's mighty popular today," says Ma, winking at me and John. "When do you plan to go on your fishing trip?"

"Early tomorrow morning," says Pa. "Soon as it's light enough to see the road. We'll be sleeping in Bill Steven's bunkhouse on the lake, cooking on a campfire, and eating all the fish we can hold. You men had better go check your tackle. If there's anything you need, we'll have to get it tonight. Once the sun comes up tomorrow morning, we're off!"

And we were! Old sleepyhead John, believe it or not, was bright-eyed and rarin' to go. We stowed everything in the car — tackle, provisions, extra clothes. Then in the misty, gray, beginning light of day, we were off!

Ma stood in the door, wavin' good-bye.

That was Saturday morning. Monday afternoon

we pulled up in front of the house with half the fish in Lake Winnewingo in our car.

I'll have to admit that we didn't catch all the fish we were carrying. Only a part of them. Seems like everybody we'd met that day, soon's they found out we were heading home, gave us all their extra fish to add to our collection.

"We're going to have a fish fry like we've never had before!" says Pa in high spirits. "We'll have all the neighbors in. It'll take half the town to eat all these fish!"

Pa set about cleaning them, and Ma started in frying fish almost as soon as we carried them into the kitchen. Glinda and Sharon ran around the neighborhood, inviting everybody to come.

After a while they reported back.

"The Sherwoods aren't back yet. Neither are the Gonzaleses."

"And Janie says her folks are going out for the evening, but she'll come."

I looked at the platters of fried fish. I'd never in my life seen so much fish asking to be eaten.

"When can we start, Ma?"

"When the guests arrive. You wash up."

Me and John, we sat in the grass with the other kids. Somebody brought a heap of hot cornbread, and somebody else brought salad fresh from their garden. Mrs. Bailey brought cream and a big bowl of berries.

"Did you ever hear of anybody bursting from eating too much?" I ask John.

"Oh, sure," he says. "Lots of times. You think you might?"

"Any minute now," I say, lying back. "I never thought I'd get a chance to eat all the fish I wanted, but I think I just have."

"Me too," says John. "I couldn't eat another fish if it walked up to me and begged."

After sunset the grown-ups sat around, talking. Ma put candles on the table, and they looked real pretty in the growing dark.

Sharon and Glinda and their friends went off to the concert in the park.

Me and John and our friend Jake, we disappeared up into the Crow's Nest and spied down on the rest of them.

"What a relaxing way to spend an evening!" says one of the men. "I can see that at-home camping has its advantages. Don't know when I've had a chance like this just to quietly watch the sun go down and the moon come up. This is the way people used to unwind after an honest day's work."

"No telephone jangling. No television blaring," says one of the women. "I'm all for it. I think *we* ought to do this next summer."

"Well, it's nice for visiting with your friends," says Ma. "We can just relax and enjoy each other's company."

"What do you do of an evening when you don't have company?"

"Why, we just sit back and enjoy the evening," says Pa, "till it gets dark. Then we go to bed. But you know, it's really the morning that's important. We get up with the sun. That's the best part of the whole day, and most people sleep through it! Hardly ever see a sunrise their whole lives long. What a waste!"

"You wouldn't believe what a person can get done in the morning before it's time to go to work," says Ma. "Makes a world of difference. Of course, I don't have to go to work every morning, only some mornings, but when I do, seems like I've finished at home before I leave. I always garden early. Always hang out the wash early. I love to be out of doors on a summer morning."

"How do you manage the laundry when the electric washing machine's not running?"

"Oh, we plunge it in a washtub like our grandmothers did. The boys are awfully good at that. They run the wash through the hand wringer for me too. Then I hang it on the line because I like to.

The girls take down the wash when it's dry and have it all put away by noon. That way it's no chore for any one person."

"What I can't understand," says one of the women, "is how you can get along without a stove. And you being a professional cook!"

"Well, I do my professional cooking at somebody else's house," says Ma. "At home I can do as I please. I'm not too fond of a hot stove in the summer, so I've worked up a lot of cold dishes that the family likes. Pa wants a hot dish now and then, so I use the pressure cooker to save cooking time. We use a camp stove, you know. For refrigeration we buy ice. The boys haul it home and put it in the freezer of the refrigerator.

"It's all a matter of habit. We've just changed our habits, haven't we, Pa?"

"And for the better," says Pa. "The thing I like best is living by the sun. That's very wholesome. Everyone could profit by it. I enjoy carpentering in the morning before I leave for work. That way the first part of the day is mine, not somebody else's."

"He's made a big, roomy closet in the girls' bedroom," says Ma, "and a built-in dressing table and bookshelves. Come around tomorrow, and I'll show you."

"Well, that's a lot more constructive than watching everything that comes on television for hours every night," says someone.

"The funny thing is," says someone else, "that any one of us could start the day when the sun comes up, but we are all in the habit of staying up half the night just because we have electric lights. And we're not likely to change our habits as long as we can turn the lights on. What you folks have done is simply to make it impossible to turn the lights on. Then everything follows from that."

"Like I said," says Pa, "it changes your life for the better. It's even got me to thinking about riding a bicycle to work instead of driving the car. I'm not doing it yet, but I'm thinking about it."

About this time Jake goes down the ladder and asks his folks if he can spend the night with us in the Crow's Nest. They agree, and Ma and Pa agree, so he does.

Next morning I was up early. Jake has a way of kicking in his sleep and throwing his arms around. The only way to get out of range of him was to get out of the tree.

Passing through the kitchen, I saw the lettuce crisper from the refrigerator sitting on the counter. It was full of dressed fish, covered with water.

"Junior!"

It was Ma.

"What are you doing up so early?" she asks. "I thought you'd be worn out."

"Jake's a very active sleeper," I say. "What's this fish doing here? I thought we ate it all."

"Not all of it," says Ma. "We don't have any freezer, you know, and it won't keep just on ice. Your Pa says there's a way to salt fish and dry it in the sun so that it will keep."

"That's interesting," I say. "Where's the salt?"

"That's salt water it's soaking in. We have to keep adding salt so there's just enough, but not too much. Salt draws the juices out of the fish. In a couple of weeks, when the fish are all struck through with salt, then we'll lay them out in the sun to finish drying."

Well, as luck would have it, when the day came to start sun-drying the fish, Jake was spending the night with us again. Naturally I was up early.

"Where will you dry the fish?" I ask Ma. "On the picnic table?"

"Unless you can think of a better place," says Ma. "The fish have to be in the shade the first day."

"How about the north roof of the woodshed?" I suggest. "It's shady up there all day."

"That's a good idea," says Ma. "Then the fish won't smell up the table. I'll put you in charge."

Pa had gathered a bunch of slats to lay the fish on. They have to have air all around them while they're drying. Before John or Jake ever stirred, I got the slats tacked up on the north roof of the woodshed.

Ma squeezed as much water as she could out of each fish with her rolling pin. Then she stood on the stepladder and held the panful of drained fish for me, up on the roof. Being very careful, I laid the fish out on the slats.

"Why does the fish have to dry in the shade the first day?" I ask her.

"So the surface won't dry too fast and keep the inside from thoroughly drying. After the fish have had a day of slow drying in the shade, then we'll put them in the sun."

"Then we can just move everything to the south roof, can't we?"

"Skat!" says Ma in a fierce voice.

I looked around, and there was the Sherwoods' big tom cat, creeping over the ridgepole of the roof. I went after it, and it left in a hurry.

"He smells that fish," says Ma. "You'd better stay up there to keep him and his friends away."

By and by John and Jake began to stir. Pretty soon they came climbing down the rope ladder.

"Hey, Junior, how come you get to be up there?" asks John.

"Oh, something special Ma's letting me do because I got up first."

"Well, now we're up, it's our turn," says John.

"Maybe," I say, sort of holding back. "But probably our guest should be first."

"Great!" says Jake. "I'll be back in a flash."

In a few minutes he was back again, still eating the last of his toast. Then it dawned on him that he didn't know what he was coming up to do.

"Fish?" he asks. "What are you doing with fish?"

I explained everything to him. John was coming up the ladder to the woodshed roof now. "Can't me and Jake both come up at the same time?" he asks.

"Well, I guess so," I say, slow. "Maybe that would work. You'll get to stay up twice as long, of course. I've been up an hour. So you'll get to stay up two hours."

"OK!" says John, eager to take over.

I scooted down the ladder and disappeared before either of them could say a word. They both thought they'd won some kind of a victory.

Two hours later I showed up again and found John and Jake down on the ground, guarding the fish from below. We spent the rest of the day doin' guard duty against the cats. More than one showed up and had to be discouraged. And then there was an old crow who was determined to outwit us. Even while we were talking right below him, he'd sneak up and try to grab a piece of fish.

"How can we guard the fish when it gets dark?" I ask Pa after dinner.

"No need to," says Pa. "We'll bring it in. No telling how much wildlife would collect tonight to save us the worry of looking after our fish."

Me and John, we climbed up on the woodshed roof, while Pa stood on the ladder and held the lettuce crisper. Ever so careful, we picked up each piece of fish with pancake turners and laid it in the crisper.

When we were through, the crisper wasn't as full of fish as it had been when I began in the morning.

"How can that be?" I ask. "We didn't let the crow nor the cats get a single piece. How come there's not as much fish?"

"There are still just as many pieces," says Pa. "But each piece is a little smaller."

"I know why!" I say. "Because they're drying out. Each piece has less water!"

"Right!" says Pa. "And tomorrow night each piece will be a little smaller still. Because of being more dried out."

"Good grief!" says John. "Do we have to do guard duty another whole day?"

I didn't tell John that there were about five more days ahead of us. "Don't worry," I say. "I've got an idea. Let's go up in the Crow's Nest and talk it over." Besides I was figuring on getting a good night's sleep for a change. Jake had gone home.

In the morning we got the kite string and then we got all the tin cans out of the kitchen trash. We rinsed out the cans and made holes in them by pounding a nail through. Then we strung the string through the holes. We drove in a nail at one end of the woodshed roof at the lower corner and tied one end of the string to it. Then we drove in another nail at the other lower corner of the roof. We bent that nail to make a loop. Through the loop we passed the string and then dropped the spool of string to the ground. We were all set to go!

We scrambled down the stepladder and grabbed the spool of string and hid in the bushes with it.

About the time we thought nothing was going to happen, down out of the sky dropped the old crow! He walked along the ridge of the roof, looking like he owned it and turning his bright little eyes this way and that, looking for an ambush. We waited till he hopped down toward a piece of fish.

Clatter! Clatter! Bang! Bang! Bang!

We gave the string a big yank, and all the tin cans banged against each other with a terrible racket!

The old crow let out a big squawk and took off in a hurry, flappin' his wings like he couldn't get airborne fast enough!

Me and John laughed till it hurt. That smart old

crow had walked right into our ambush!

"Now it's time for the Cat Invasion," says John.

"I'm going to get the chessmen," I say, "and the chessboard. We can take turns watching the roof. Whoever has just moved can watch for cats."

Well, we ambushed cats for the rest of the week, until the fish were completely dried out. The old crow never did come back. The last day only one cat showed up, one that we'd never seen before. Ma and the girls kept us supplied with lemonade and cookies and sandwiches. Once in a while Sharon and Glinda would take over to let us go swimming. Twice we convinced Jake to come back and help us operate the Tin Can Terror Machine.

"I think this fish is perfectly dry," says Pa one evening.

Me and John, we whooped and hollered and raced around til we couldn't stand up.

Ma wrapped the dried salt fish in plastic and stowed it on a kitchen shelf. From time to time she makes chowder of it. It's first-rate fish chowder, and me and John, we always think about how we did guard duty against the cats and the smart old crow.

Tape 8

Tale
of
a Comet

Then came the night when we set the alarm clock for midnight and went to sleep on the grass.

John wasn't about to wake up when the alarm went off. He groaned and rolled over.

"Hey! There's a big one! John! Wake up! Look! There's another! Hurry!"

I kept shaking him, and finally he began to come to.

"Look, John! Good grief, all you have to do is open your eyes! You don't have to move another muscle. Quick! There goes another one!"

He sure was missing a lot! I kept wondering how he could sleep through anything so terrific.

Finally he came to life, rubbing his eyes and

yawning and pulling a blanket around him while he sat up.

"Hey, look at *that!*" he yells, pointing. "A real falling star! All across the sky! Did you see that?"

"That's what I've been telling you for the last half-hour," I say. "You've missed a whole bunch of them. Keep looking. That last one was Number Sixteen. I'm going to set up the camera."

I went to the picnic table. On top of the table I had left a stool. On the stool I had left the camera in a plastic bag.

"Why don't you use the flashlight?" asks John.

"Can't," I reply. "My eyes would have to get used to the dark all over again. Anyhow I know what I'm doing in the dark."

I felt for the plastic bag. It was dry. That meant that the dew wouldn't cloud the camera lens as long as it was on top of the stool on top of the table.

I had a rubber band ready. I fastened down the shutter lever of the camera with the rubber band and, careful, laid the camera down on its back with the lens pointing at the sky. Then I went back to where John was.

"How can you leave the shutter open," asks John, "without spoiling the film?"

"Oh, there's not enough light to do that. Only the meteors will leave a trace. The film is sitting there ready to record any meteor whenever it falls."

"You'll sure have a lot of meteor tracks in one picture!"

"For sure. We'll get it enlarged and hang it on the wall of our room."

We lay back and watched. What a show! After about Number Forty, we got in an argument and lost count.

"Where are all these falling stars coming from?" asks John.

"They're not stars. They're just little particles about as big as the end of your finger."

"But how come we can see them 'way up in the sky?"

"Because they catch fire soon as they hit the atmosphere of the Earth. Like striking a match. Only the friction is from striking the air."

"Wow! They're really going fast! How fast, do you think?"

"About a hundred times as fast as a rifle bullet."

"What if one hit us?"

"Oh, it couldn't do that," I say. "It's too little. It burns up before it gets down to Earth."

"Look at that one!" says John. "It went down into those trees behind Jake's house!"

"No, it didn't. It fell out of our sight behind those trees. It's still in the upper atmosphere."

"Bet you!" says John.

"How much?" I say, quick. "A roll of film?"

"You're on!" says John, and we shook on it.

"You'll have to prove it fell," I say. "You'll have to find the meteorite."

"Don't worry. I will. I saw exactly where it fell."

John gets these notions that he's right when he's dead wrong. Like once a long time ago, he said he could catch some light in a box and take it into a dark closet and open the box, and the light would come out so you could see it. He said he'd already done it. So one day we spent all morning catching light in a box and crowding into our clothes closet and opening the box, over and over. I never did see any light come out, but John always claimed he could. Pa says he has a hyperactive imagination. Anyway I let him think he could find a meteorite. Sometimes there's no use arguing with him. I knew I had me a new roll of film if he paid up.

"You didn't say where these little meteors are coming from," says John.

"They're from the tail of a comet. Every summer the Earth orbits across the tail of this comet, and then we can see these meteor showers."

"Where's the comet?"

"Oh, it's orbiting the sun in a cockeyed way. One of these years we'll get to see it when it comes in sight. I think it's 1983."

"Wow! We can't miss that!"

"We won't," I say. "In the meantime we can

watch the Perseid meteor showers every summer."

"Is that the name of the comet?"

"No, Perseus is that constellation over there." I pointed to the northeast. "It just *looks* like the meteor showers come from Perseus, but they don't really. They come from the comet, like I said."

"What's the comet called?"

"Swift-Tuttle, after the two men who discovered it."

But John wasn't listening. He interrupted me. "Swift Turtle! I get it—it's going fast, but it seems slow. Like the turtle that won the race."

"Swift-*Turtle*?" I say, but then I stop. John can be real comical sometimes without knowing it. I didn't correct him. I don't think I ever will. I just like to think of a comet as a Swift Turtle, plowin' through space at its own pace. I have a real liking for comets.

"Maybe someday I'll discover a comet of my own," I say. "I've always hoped I could."

"What would you name it?" asks John.

"Pokey Antelope," I say, trying not to laugh. I rolled over and stuffed the blanket in my mouth, but I couldn't choke back the laugh, and it broke out. I couldn't stop.

"Hey, stop cackling!" says John, not getting the joke. "You'll wake up the whole neighborhood."

I simmered down after a while and was lying on

my back, puffing, when I saw a great enormous burst of blue light. It lasted about twenty seconds and then it was gone. It didn't make a sound.

"What was *THAT?*" says John.

I was speechless. The thing that kept coming into my head was that it was a comet exploding when it hit the Earth's atmosphere. Finally I told John.

"You mean old Swift Turtle blew up? *How* about that?" says John in amazement. "Would I ever like to have a picture of that!"

I grabbed him. I was so excited I couldn't even talk. I ran to the picnic table, reached up, and, ever so careful, I slipped the rubber band off the shutter. I slipped the camera into the plastic bag and left it on the stool out of reach of the dew.

"What's the matter?" asks John when I came back.

"Nothing's the matter," I say. "There's just a good possibility that we *do* have a picture of that comet explosion!"

We could hardly wait for the days to pass until our film was developed and printed. When the day finally came to pick it up, we were there as soon as Mr. Green opened his drugstore.

"Your photo prints?" he says. "Those must be extra special pictures—you're so anxious to get them."

"Just one of 'em, Mr. Green," I say. "I think we've got a very important shot of a comet exploding."

"Oh, that's right," says Mr. Green. "Jake's been telling me what an astronomer you are. Well, here they are — your prints."

I grabbed them, and John's eyes were as close to them as mine. My hands weren't working as smooth as they should, and I nearly dropped the whole bunch of prints, taking them out of the envelope. I flipped through the stack.

"There it is!" says John.

And there it was! A perfect shot!

Even Mr. Green was impressed. "You boys ought to take that photo around to the newspaper office. Mr. Shea might be glad to have a look at it."

"Wow!" says John, and we headed for *The Bugle* office.

Mr. Shea looked at the comet picture. Then he pulled his glasses off his forehead and had another look.

"Boys, this is a very interesting photo you've got here. Tell me again about how you took it."

We told him the whole story again.

"I'd like to check with an astronomer at the University," he says, picking up the phone.

Then he told the story over the phone. When he hung up, he had a big grin on his face. "Dr. Rowell is coming over to have a look at your photo. He seems to think it might be something else, not a comet."

"What could it be?" I ask.

"Let's wait and see what he says. Why don't you fellas go buy a couple of ice cream cones while you're waiting?" And he hands us some coins from his pocket. "Don't stay too long. Dr. Rowell may want to question you."

We thanked Mr. Shea and ran. It didn't take us long at all to load up with a butter pecan cone and a double fudge. When we got back, Dr. Rowell was just walking in.

Mr. Shea handed him the photo. He studied it a minute and then he looked at me and John.

"What color was it?"

"Blue," we both said at once.

"Which one is the astronomer?" he asks.

I stepped forward.

"You've taken a remarkable picture," he says, "but it's not a comet."

"What is it then?" I ask, completely baffled.

"A satellite."

"Exploding?"

"Exactly. Igniting as it enters the atmosphere. Just as the meteor particles do. As a matter of fact, you may have the only photograph of the event. We've had a number of phone calls and letters from people who saw it, but no photographs. Sounds like a front-page story, doesn't it?" he added, smiling at Mr. Shea.

"Well now, while we're all here together," says Mr. Shea, "let's just have a general discussion, and I'll write down the facts."

So he asked the questions and did the writing, and we did the talking, me and John and Dr. Rowell.

When it was all over, Dr. Rowell invited me and John to go back to the observatory with him and look at the big telescope close up. We did, and it was the best time I've ever had in my whole life!

When we got home, everybody was at the table, eating dinner. But they all stopped eating when we told our story.

"A satellite!" says Pa, slapping his leg. "Why, we've got a couple of Space-Age Heroes here at the table with us!"

"How about some Satellite Stew?" says Ma, filling up our plates.

That was only the beginning. *The Bugle* printed our photo of the satellite exploding, on the front page, too. And below it was a picture of me and John and my telescope. And the whole story was there.

That's not the end either, because then we started getting phone calls and letters from people who'd read about it. The best letter was from Dr. Rowell. He said that in recognition of our good work, he was ordering a mount for my telescope—you know, a stand to hold it up!

And that's not the end either. It's just the beginning of some real serious work in astronomy for me. Anything can happen now!

The Under- ground Secret

Me and John, we were hankering for a new place to live—somewhere where we'd never lived before. Not a tree, not a tent.

Then one morning while we were weeding the garden, we hit on an idea and right off we realized that it would have to be a secret. If anybody discovered it, sure as shootin' they'd put a stop to it. So we were very careful to cover our tracks.

"Ma," says Sharon bright and early one morning when she was drying her hair in the sun, "why is it that the boys moved their tent around behind the woodshed?"

"Why, to keep cool, dearie," says Ma, busy in the garden. "They said they were moving to the north side of the woodshed to keep cool."

"But they don't sleep there," says Sharon.

"No?"

"No. They're sleeping in the Crow's Nest."

"Well, that's all right," says Ma.

"I think something's going on," says Sharon, and she went in the house.

John nudged me. We were up in the Crow's Nest, listening. We waited until Ma went in and then we scooted down the rope ladder and ran behind the woodshed.

We were digging us a cave there.

We had to hide the hole we were digging, so we pitched the tent over it. We had a system of loosening the ropes on one side and leaning the tent over on the fence while we were digging the cave.

Then we had the problem of where to hide the dirt that we were digging up. We were piling it against the woodshed and covering it with leafy boughs, but we knew that wouldn't work forever. We hoped that we could think of a better way later.

Digging a cave is terrible hard work.

Me and John, we kept up our spirits by talking about what we'd do in our cave, once we got it finished. We'd fix up some kind of a hidden entrance, so no one else could find it. We'd have to use candles in it because it would be pitch black. We'd have bunks in it and sleep there. We'd line the walls and floor with bricks so we wouldn't be breathing dirt all the time. There were some old bricks in the woodshed that Pa was saving to make an outdoor fireplace with. He never talks about it any more, so we figured he probably wouldn't miss them if we made use of them.

One thing we weren't sure of was how to hold the roof up. But we had plenty of time to figure that out, because first we had to get the cave dug.

We took turns digging. One of us would dig with the garden spade, and the other would patrol the back yard, in case anybody came out. For one thing, Pa had taken to riding his bicycle to work, so we couldn't hear him drive up. The bushes along the fence hid us on one side, and the woodshed hid us on the other side.

We had special digging clothes that we put on, so's Ma wouldn't suspect. We figured on using them over and over and then just washing them once when we were through with them. We did an awful lot of washing up in the shower, but no one caught on.

"I don't think we're *ever* going to finish this cave," says John one Saturday afternoon. He'd just finished spade duty and was sitting down, sweating. "Look at it! It's only three feet deep and not big enough for even one bunk, much less two! Good grief! I've never worked so hard in my life, and what have we got to show for it?"

"It's an awful good hole," I say. "We shouldn't waste it. Maybe we could make something else out of it."

"Like what?"

"I don't know," I say, discouraged. "What good is a hole if it isn't a cave?"

Suddenly we realized that we'd made a big mistake.

We'd let down our guard! Somebody was out in the backyard! Quick as a flash, we hauled up the tent. I was covering up the fresh dirt, while John skinned out of his digging clothes, when round the corner of the woodshed came Pa!

"Here you are!" he says. "I just brought home a watermelon like you never saw before! Let's take care of it!"

"Wow!" I say to attract attention while John skidoos for the shower before Pa can get a good look at him.

"What's the matter with him?" asks Pa, starting to sit down in the doorway of the tent.

"Hey, Pa!" I yell. "I wouldn't do that if I were you!"

I was too late.

Next thing I knew, Pa was falling in, and the tent was collapsing on top of him. All I could do was stand there and try to figure out where Pa was, under all that churning green canvas.

"Here, Pa," I say. "This way out. No, over here."

Well, after a lot of quaking of the tent and some very strange sounds from Pa, he emerged.

"What in blue blazes are you trying to do, Junior?" he roars. "Is this a trap of some kind you've dug here?"

"No, Pa, it's a cave," I say, blurting it out.

"Well, why in tarnation didn't you tell me?"

"I tried to, Pa, but you sat down too quick."

"Down is right," says Pa. "Let's see what your cave looks like." And he began hauling away at the collapsed pile of tent.

I helped, and I've got to say that he'd done a real good job of pulling out every stake and thrashing the whole thing into a fizzle. After a lot of tugging, we got the tent and the rigging pulled to one side.

"Why, that's a right good beginning!" says Pa, looking at our cave.

"How long do you think it'll take us to finish it, Pa?"

"Maybe by the end of next summer."

"Oh, ghorm!" I moan and sit down. "We were counting on living in it *this* summer."

John came back while we were talking, all clean and shining. With one look he took in that the secret was out.

"Now look here, men," says Pa. "You've done a fine lot of work here. But you've only just begun. You're maybe one-tenth done. And once you've finished, say the end of next summer, you're going to discover that you don't want to live down there after all."

"Why not?" asks John.

"Because you'll be eating dirt all the time."

"But we'll line it with bricks!"

"Do you have any idea of what bricks will cost you?"

"Why, we were figuring on using the bricks in the woodshed." I didn't dare say, "The ones you were saving for an outdoor fireplace."

But Pa didn't even bring that up.

"Those bricks won't be one-fourth enough," he says. "Let's think about this. Maybe there's something else that you can make out of your cave. Something that you could finish this summer."

"Another thing," says John. "What can we do with all the dirt?" He pulled off the boughs to show Pa how much there was.

"Why, that's it!" cries Pa, slapping his leg. "That's the clue to the whole thing!"

Me and John, we couldn't see any clue.

"Did you fellas ever hear of a rammed-earth wall?"

We shook our heads.

"Well, it's a method as old as the hills for making walls out of dirt. You use a wooden form that's the thickness of the walls you want and you ram dirt into it hard enough so that when you take away the wooden frame, the dirt holds up. Like unbaked brick."

"You mean it wouldn't crumble?"

"Guaranteed not to," says Pa.

"But, Pa, what would we want walls for?"

"That's a good question," says Pa, and he stopped. After a minute he says. "It would make a good root cellar."

"Why would anyone want a cellar for roots?"

"Root *vegetables*—like potatoes and carrots and beets and onions. A cellar to store them in, where it's cool in summer and above freezing in winter."

"For Ma's garden vegetables!" I say. "She could store her root vegetables in it!"

"That's it!" says Pa, getting up. "That's the answer! We figured it out in our own think tank!"

"We ought to keep it a secret," says John, "for her birthday."

"Best idea yet," says Pa. "Now how about that watermelon?"

So we spent the rest of the afternoon on the watermelon. Me and John, we saved our seeds to plant next spring.

Pa made us a wooden form to put the dirt in. And he made a flat piece of wood with a long handle on it that fitted neatly inside the form. That was to ram with.

Me and John, we squared our hole and made the floor even. Then we started on the rammed-earth walls.

If there's anything that takes more muscle than digging a cave, it's ramming earth walls. We took turns at it, scooping dirt into the wooden form and then ramming it down till it was hard as rock almost. Then we'd move the form to another place and start all over again. After a while we got the hang of it, and every evening we'd have more wall to show Pa.

We took Sharon and Linda in on our secret so that they would keep Ma from coming behind the woodshed.

We made the walls about three feet high. Then we laid boards across the top and tar paper over the boards. We covered the boards and the tar paper over with a good layer of dirt.

Pa enlarged Ma's garden and gave us the grass sod that he dug up. We laid it on the roof. Then we piled loose dirt on the ground against the outside of the rammed-earth walls, so that they slanted

outward. We covered them with sod too. That's so the rain won't wash any of it away. We were lucky that it didn't rain while we were building it.

"The pioneers on the prairie lived in houses like this," says John. "We could build *us* a sod house if we wanted to."

"For sure," I say. "Just like this one, only bigger. Sure we could do it."

We had left an opening in one wall for the door. We dug steps down to the floor level, which was three feet underground. We laid bricks on the dirt steps.

Pa built a narrow little door frame and two narrow little doors. They fitted into the door frame, one on the inside and one on the outside, with a dead air space between them. That was for insulation. The doors didn't open on hinges, because there wasn't room. Instead they had to be lifted out. Pa said we wouldn't have to do it often, only when we were storing vegetables or getting them out.

Last of all, we laid the bricks on the floor.

"Do you think you'll be finished in time?" asks Glinda. "Tomorrow's Ma's birthday."

"You keep her from findin' out what we're doing, and we'll finish it," says John, "even if we have to stay up all night."

What we did instead was we got up early the next morning and put the finishing touches on.

Then we sat back and looked at our root cellar. We could hardly believe that it was really finished.

"It's hard to think back to when we weren't working on it," I say. "Seems like we've been doing it for years."

"It's solid as rock," says John. "Going to stand for years, Pa says. You know, I've *never* felt so good about anything we've ever built before!" And he punches me on the shoulder.

I punched him back, and we went in to wish Ma a happy birthday and to wait for the right minute to tell her.

Tape 10

The
Winners

Ma was overcome with surprise.

"Never in my life," she says, *"never* have I had a present that I liked better! How did you ever think of it?"

"We got the idea from Pa," says John.

"I got the idea from John and Junior," says Pa.

"Well, I think you all three deserve credit for it," says Ma. "My goodness! How much work you boys have put into it!"

"It'll last for years, Ma," I say.

"It'll last forever," says Pa, "short of an earthquake. I understand that somebody's going to build some shelves for you, too."

"Oh, that will be dandy!" says Ma.

"Can we keep vegetables in it all winter?" asks Glinda.

"We'll test it this winter and find out," says Pa. "We can also use it for storing things in the summer, to keep them cool. Not ice cold, but cool."

"That's right," says John. "It's real cool inside. Come on down. I'll show you."

So one by one, everybody goes down to see how cool Ma's new root cellar is.

"Time for pancakes!" says Sharon, and she scoots off to the kitchen.

We had breakfast at the picnic table under the trees. Sharon and Glinda cooked it and served it, and Ma didn't have to get up once from the table.

"Oh, I almost forgot," says Ma. "I have a surprise for you too! Junior, would you run in and get the envelope on my dresser? And my glasses too, please?"

I made it in on the double and got back before anybody had a chance to say anything important. I gave Ma her glasses and the envelope.

We were all watching her and wondering. Out of the envelope she took two pieces of paper. One was a clipping from a newspaper.

"I'll read this first," she says, taking up the newspaper article. And this is what she reads:

PRIZE OFFERED
FOR ENERGY CONSERVATION IDEA

Mr. Aldon Bates, well-known local businessman, has announced a prize of $100 to be awarded to the person of this community who submits the best idea for the conservation of energy.

"The President," said Mr. Bates, "has laid on the shoulders of every patriotic citizen a responsibility that we should be quick to assume: To seek out ways of saving energy. In order to stimulate thinking and enterprise in this direction, I am offering a cash prize of $100 for the best idea to be submitted before Labor Day."

Judges will be Dr. Charles Engles of the Department of Physics at the University, Miss Jesse Stacy, teacher of home economics at Chrisman High School, and Mr. Samuel Shea, editor of *The Bugle*.

Those intending to enter the contest should mail their ideas to ENERGY, Bates Manufacturing Company, 1100 North Main Street. Only letters received before Labor Day can be considered.

"Now," says Ma, "it seems to me that somebody in this family might have a $100 idea!"

"Wow!" me and John say together.

"Why, the root cellar!" says Sharon. "That's an energy-saving idea! It's an outdoor summer cooler that doesn't take any energy, just the cool of the earth. And in winter it keeps things from freezing with the *warmth* of the earth."

"You're absolutely right," says Ma. "Any other ideas?"

"The camp stove," says Glinda. "It doesn't use electricity nor gas, either one. Only a little fuel oil now and then. And it's so much trouble that we don't cook on it very much at all. That's sure a good saving of energy."

"And the washing machine, Ma," I say. "We don't use it *nor* the dryer. Dryers take a lot of electricity."

"And the telephone!" puts in Glinda. "We haven't had one all summer."

Ma is smiling now. She turns to Glinda and says, "Now, dearie, tell me. Have you really minded not having a telephone all summer?"

Everybody laughs and looks at Glinda.

"Well, actually, no," says Glinda. "Because all my friends come to see me instead of just phoning. So really, it's better. And if I have to phone, I can go up the street to the pay phone."

"Did anybody mind not having electric lights at night?" asks Ma.

"Not me," I say. "Me and John, we just got up earlier. Right around sunrise is one of the best parts of the day. Nobody to bother you, and it's cool. I wouldn't have missed that for anything."

"Did anybody miss hot water?"

Sharon and Glinda looked at each other. John beamed.

"Not really," says Sharon. "I like cold showers now. And I know they're good for you. The thing

I really missed at first was the electric hair dryer, but I got used to not having it. I just dried my hair in the sun and I think it's getting lighter, more yellow."

"What I missed most," says Glinda, "was the electric hair curler, but I went back to curlers and pins, and they work all right."

"I'm still waiting to hear the $100 idea," says Pa. "Which one of these brilliant energy-saving ideas is the best?"

There was a pause in the conversation.

"Why couldn't we lump them all together?" says John. "They all came about because we turned off the utilities."

"Aha!" says Ma and she picked up the other piece of paper. When she unfolded it, we could see that it was a letter.

"Dear Mr. Bates," she reads. "We hereby submit the following energy-saving idea:

"Our family had the utilities disconnected for the summer—electricity, gas, telephone. (We did not have the water disconnected.)

"We found that we could get along without a great many things that we thought we were dependent on and we have even enjoyed being free of them. We experienced the fun of camping at home. Living was simpler, and we saved the money

we would have spent on three months of utilities.

"Best of all, instead of needlessly squandering energy, we saved it.

"We recommend this idea to every American family that wants to save energy and money and have some good pioneer fun."

Ma looked round at all of us. "Then I signed the names of all you children. Pa and I think that you should have all the credit—and the money, if you win."

"That was a very good letter, Ma," says John. "I never realized that we did all that."

"Me neither," I say. "When will you send the letter in?"

"Oh, I've already sent in in," says Ma. "Labor Day is next week, you know. What I've got here is just a copy."

"I can't believe that we'd ever win," says Glinda.

"I can't believe that you won't," says Pa. "Can you think of a better idea?"

"How about the way you stopped driving the car to work and ride a bicycle?" asks Sharon.

"Other people are doing that," says Pa. "To win a contest you have to be way out in front."

There was a loud knocking at the front door. I ran to see who it was.

"A man from Mr. Shea's newspaper," I say, out of breath when I get back.

"Invite him to come out here to the backyard," says Pa.

So I led the man around to the backyard.

Pa stood up.

"I'm George Lane from *The Bugle*," says the man, holding out his hand. "Mr. Alton Bates asked

me to follow up a very interesting submission that
was made to his contest by four people at this ad-
dress, named Junior and John and Sharon and
Glinda."

"Well, you came at the right time," says Pa.
"You've got them all here together." And he intro-
duces us to Mr. Lane.

Mr. Lane was young and friendly and he began
chatting with us right off.

"You know what I'd like to do?" he says after a
few minutes. "I'd like to have a real in-depth inter-
view with one of you. I'll come back every morning
about this time with a tape recorder until we get the
whole story."

"With just one of us?" asks John.

Mr. Lane nodded.

"Which one?" asks Ma.

"The youngest one," he says, looking at me.

"Why me?" I ask in amazement.

"I think it might be more interesting to the read-
ers from your point of view."

"How about that?" says John, punching me.

I was too surprised to punch him back.

But we did it, me and Mr. Lane and the tape recorder. It turned out to be fun.

This book is what I said on the tapes.

Oh yes, and me and John, we each opened a sav-
ings account at the bank with twenty-five dollars.

And so did Sharon and Glinda. Pa was right. We did win the contest.

"Just look," says Glinda, "how we appreciate having hot water and electric lights and all those things, now that the utilities are back on! I don't think I ever appreciated them before. But now I could never take things like that for granted, not ever again. Think how many people in the world go without them all their lives! Now we know how *they* feel. I think it's a very important thing to know."

"How right you are!" says Pa. "I think we'll all agree that it has been a broadening experience. And just as we appreciate going back to winter living, so we're going to enjoy changing to camping life again next summer."

"You mean we can do it again next summer?" me and John ask together.

"Absolutely!" says Pa. "Any life that has as much to offer as camping-at-home should be repeated again and again."

Me and John began whoopin' and hollerin' and punchin' each other all over the place.

"Hey!" says John, stopping all of a sudden. "What about those snowshoes, Pa? The ones you promised us if the camping turned out to be fun. Remember?"

"Comes the first snowfall," says Pa, "you'll have them. They'll keep you fit for camping until next summer rolls around!"